Poems from Underground

Paul F Blackburn

PreeTa ✳ **Press**

Foreword

Anyone who has encountered the phenomenal force of nature that is Paul Blackburn will not forget the experience in a hurry - or possibly ever. Even if they try very, very hard.

You may have heard Paul perform his songs in the endearingly off-the-wall way that only he can. (Which is perhaps just as well.)

Maybe you have witnessed him deliver his poems and stories to enthusiastic, and occasionally bemused, audiences here in the UK, in Europe or - as he often reminds people - the USA.

Once upon a time, you may even have glimpsed Paul on TV as a young, Northern poet in the early days of Channel 4. Possibly, you have witnessed him attempt to play a teapot, or endeavour to dance with a brush as a member of an avant garde, postmodern multi-media music group.

I am proud to say that I have been privy to all these happenings, and indeed many more not suitable for public consumption
Anarchic poet, songwriter and chronicler of the absurd, psychedelic philosopher, master of Dada and expert exponent of the surreal, there is only one Paul Blackburn. Or is there?

His various incarnations have been legion: school drop-out, political activist, working-class hippy, committed iconoclast, key contributor to the ground-breaking Bolton Free Press, founder member of national poetry network, Write Out Loud and most recently Chair of the Bolton Arts organization Live From Worktown. Like Trump's tan, Paul has many layers.

However, Paul's main thrust has always been his own original writing and here within this book is a small sample of his work.
Paul's poems pull the rug out from under your feet and will challenge you to think differently. The current collection ranges from the comically complex to the deeply tragic, sometimes all in the same sentence.

Having the capacity to see the world afresh, drawing on a rare combination of childlike wonder and sophisticated understanding, Paul presents the reader with a unique and often provocative take on life.

I have known Paul for most of my adult life and have been privileged to witness his transformation from angry young man to equally angry old man. All of the poems in this volume will take you on some kind of journey. Open up your mind: it's a trip you'll enjoy and one you'll remember.

One day back in the far-off sixties, Paul blasted off for outer space and rumour has it that he never really came back.
With this collection you can follow Paul down the rabbit hole.

You may be gone quite some time.

Dr Nat Clare

For rebels everywhere!

Acknowledgements:

'To be a condom' first appeared in Citizen 32

'Damned Love,' 'Last train to Shitsville',
'Schrodinger's Poet', 'Corporate Thinking' and
'Freedom' appeared in International Times

Front cover design based on a photograph by
Thurston Hopkins

Back cover photograph by Darren Thomas

Pictures for 'Freedom' & 'Schrodinger's Poet' by
Nick Victor

Published in 2017 by
Preeta Press, Bolton,
Greater Manchester
preetapress.com

ISBN: 978-1-9998489-1-0

Printed by Printdomain Ltd,

CONTENTS

Burnt sacrifice

She was as wild as the ice, sunlit springtime
A soft furnace of eyes spread the heat
No noble breast pounds like her lovers'
Together the circles complete

It's a pattern the art for the fusing
Their hands are clasped like a vice
Entwined on the altar of promise
Their love is the burnt sacrifice

Your Smile

It was your smile that first attacked me
I was decimated in the force of it
And your hair hung-down and moving
It shook me. It shook me!

It was your smile that first enwrapped me
I was corrupted in the feel of it
And your face shone golden, golden!
The very halo of your smile

It was your smile that first entrapped me
Caged me in the nap of it
And down deep thundered, thundered
The wellings of Mount Etna

It was your smile that first attached me
Umbilical in the join of it
And it is your smile that still remains
Branded in here, in here!

George Porpoise

George Porpoise loitered
without purpose. Lolloped, titanically
without a mission-statement
but blissfully definite
"I say George?"
"Yes" he seemed to answer,
though to Mr Megan the static could have been
electric gumboils, electrocuting Martians
ra-ta-ta-tat ra-ta-ta-tat
Rah Rah, ratatouille

George leapt joyously into Mr Megan's open skillet
"Don't kill it, don't kill it!"
George poised for a laugh
Crackled and snapped
Bit the decals clean off
Decamped to the naff
And was gone in a flash

George Porpoise Or was it Tortoise?
"Tortoise? Did someone say Tortoise?"
"I once had a tortoise
wore yellow, crocodile wallpaper
but couldn't squawk, tellingly."
Accidentally posted to Leicester

To Be a Condom

I wonder what it would be like
I wonder if it would be nice
I wonder if it's quite a life
To be a condom

In places that are warm and dark
Stopping things before they start
At attention, on alert
I am a condom

You can roll me on, or blow me up
I taste disgusting if you should suck
If I'm defective then that's tough luck
Dubious condom

A sentinel to guard your parts
Disguise your veins and hide the warts
A guardian against love hurts
Heroic condom

And when you're done I'm thrown away
A forlorn bag of used sperm spray
I'll never rise another day
A trash heap condom

My Window Box

My window box is a microcosm of my world
mini-titans vie to darwin
other skittle creatures

The sun is a great red plosive
clouds erupting
cascading life

A violet woman lies abed
and moans
Sweat bubbles a beard of bees
miracles crawling through her
in great tsunamis

I remember the time of snows
wild showerings
on mattress drifts
bringing their silences and fear

I crawl in
terror
at the mystery of it all

The water-colour version
of a life
where leaves collect in gangs
across hostile pavements
clocks tick out the sniff of
aging, aging…

From multiple horizons
zoom-in again and again
to
my window box
a microcosm of my world

One of your best assets

Christmas always seems so crass a way
To kiss commercialism's ass
So I'd like to kiss your's instead

Last train to Shitsville

On the last train to Shitsville
fake leopard skin sneakers
a flat cap (fucking hell!)

Girls on the way back
playing clips from
their mint concert
on limited digital camera
phones
"Remember that, kid?"

Last chance to get off.
but I'm on the last train

with
muttering invisibles
bubbling in
cartoon voices
intense word sounds
meaningless
but urgent

Orange light streaks
collide with silver-shred
tangled shots
of young & lovely
loud, laughing mouthful
perfect, cloud-teeth
falling into
aisles of reality

"We need to be moving"
it's still mental-land
in Shitsville
or what they call normal
the fuckers.

Giggling girls
shout and gambol
"will you get off…"
If only I could
no more stations but this one
last train to Shitsville..

Damned Love

Saxophones wheeze cracked on
emphysema blues smack
taking me back to
the days of cast iron
men with rail-road tracked
faces hack-coughing bar-room wisdom
or bollocking froth
drinking fuelled black velvet
and Jameson
While snap-Henry jeered at them
their liquid addiction
he smoking joints of pure black
beaten
for his honesty and look
as keen-Eddie drove past in an
American Jeep, beeped, waved
disappeared...
chased by dumb cops too stupid
to think about road blocks or call up
non-existent helicopters
...never to be seen again
except by lunatics and visionaries
wearing 3-D coloured popsicles

Saxophone poops, farts out
an odorous dissonance the

Captain himself could have blown
when the late Dave scoots in, winks
smiles his most conspiratorial saying:
'The past is a dangerous place.'
mouths something about poetry
some other shit I don't wanna hear
buys a chocolateless cappuccino
white-worm coloured
pours it down off handedly
I tell him I don't know the why
or what of it
I'm not sure I care
he agrees
after all
it's only the future
and energy levels are low

Saxophones honk spurt
kissing youth another
time
who themselves are inventing
persona's whilst fashioning
novel styles that will shortly be sold back to them
if their thoughts had been re-processed by
imagineless
industry so-called creatives
leeching whilst drinking
unpronounceable liquids made

for them by teams of cocktail imagineers
who live in low rent apartments
or squat in derelict districts
soon to be gentrified by the fuckers
they serve.

Saxophones squawk in panic
warning
the love activists of imminent
apocalypse
as the riot squad or whatever
media friendly name they are
calling themselves today
boot-stamp inadequately protected
homeless
out of empty buildings
take them to courts where
dislocated, funnel-brained judges
disallow homeless protests on the grounds
those who haven't been involved
in communities have no validity
for their actions, as if
that made any sense
at all
Judges, who don't themselves ever
have to walk past hopelessness,
except maybe to burn £50 notes
incarcerate heedlessly

defenders of the weak and powerless.
Saxophones crash, spark
wildly Bird inspired solos of
righteous indignation trusting
truth will be revealed
to us all except
midnight Jim wandering wonkily
searching for that big
fag-end and wonder pint
that will make his day
perhaps even
changing his and all
our ways...
Play Coltrane Play

The Canonisation

The light fades - it's as simple as that
The light fades
And as her eyelids close she sees eyes looking at her
They are smiling eyes!

She doesn't know if they are a reflection of her own
eyes
somehow mirrored
Or the image of other eyes that were once that close

The eyes disappear for her eyelids have
involuntarily
Opened
There is some light lingering in the darkness
She looks at a man - her lover - sleeping by her side
Oddly, she feels a trickle of sweat run down her
forehead
Odd because it isn't even warm

She leans forward to view him more closely but he
doesn't stir
She withdraws leaving him to slumber on

Lying flat on the floor
Breathing deep and rhythmically
Her eyes fixed upon an invisible point on the ceiling
She is perfectly relaxed

She perceives, without panic, that she is
disintegrating

Her consciousness is dulled and numb.
She is stilled and obliterated by the coma of the
moment
She becomes nothing and everything

Then, as mysteriously as the origins of life itself,
She is re-born and begins the lonely struggle back
Back to a new reality
Another night has groaned to a minor miracle
Another circle has completed itself

A Good Life?

Norbert Blinghammer had lived many lives
one hundred and twenty seven
to be precise
he claimed.

He had regressed and experienced them all
apparently
but was devastated to discover
that none of them
human or otherwise
had been a 'good life'

He determined this would change
and resolved that this one
his latest
would be it
the good life.

Unfortunately, he was eighty-three
when he made this decision
and died shortly
afterwards

I guess we'll have to wait for his next
human reincarnation
to find out

Freedom

The sky was a vomit green
and I felt good as
a sickly winter sun
wrestled off its night clothes
to grin a fevered beat

I picked a corner table
at an outside café
a scalding coffee
seething
hostile in an open mug

A feral stranger strode purposefully
came and sat
right by me
looked me in the eye
downed my cup in one

Disdainfully he said,
I have the freedom to do that!
I admit I was impressed
I looked at him, smiling
and I have the freedom to ...
You have the freedom to complete the poem

Who's with you now?

Is there someone else in your life
Since I threw you in the street
My bed seems fairly empty
Without you between the sheets

We'd been together so long
I got to hate your guts
That's why I poked you in the eye
And tried to cut you up

Oh they might say it's ABH
I know it was assault
But when I saw your glassy eyes
I knew it was your fault

Is there someone else in your life
Too late I find I care
I live in desolation
Without you, my teddy bear

Corporate Thinking

<Company Logo here>

This Poem is sponsored by

This Poem is sponsored by
This Poem is sponsored by
This Poem is sponsored by
This Poem is sponsored by

This Poem is sponsored by
This Poem is sponsored by
This Poem is sponsored by
This Poem is sponsored by

This Poem is sponsored by
This Poem is sponsored by
This Poem is sponsored by
This Poem is sponsored by

This Poem is sponsored by
This Poem is sponsored by
This Poem is sponsored by
This Poem is sponsored by

This Poem is sponsored by
This Poem is sponsored by
This Poem is sponsored by
This Poem is sponsored by

<Company Name and Details here>

<Company Name> is a Supporter of the Arts

Death and the boiled egg

you read the tea leaves
attempting to discern
why
your father
seemingly healthy
died, abruptly
without warning

discovered his last meal was
a boiled egg
and speculated
on its culpability

some of us do the same
in the face of inexplicable
happenstance

Searching for meaning
a talisman
perhaps
to find some kind of closure
or, under-sided, selfishly
looking for an
avoidance strategy

to assemble
information
enough
to trick
the sickleman

how tragic

Forever you will never
think of him
without the ectoplasm of a boiled egg
materialising

and whether preferences for eggs be
poached, fried, scrambled or simply boiled
we'll all soon
be
brown bread

Echo Town

As the shadows guillotine the square
this town, home an hour ago
isn't any more.
Though my echoes
are embedded here.

My itinerant, Irish grandfather
flitting across the borough
in desperate black-backed moonlight
until industrially embedded
family locked

Young woman makes tears
shaking with anxiety
whipping past the skate-park
she's not quite got her ipod sync'd
downloads fucked
feels
echos of invisibles passing
out of the box, out of her box

Women I had taken to be shoppers
three hours benched
hopeless
murmuring echoes
of comforting home-songs
crocked!

Jackboy cycles d-money
wired, brakeless
 pedals recklessly
dreaming of crack
gun-guy, bling-kings
echoes of the rap-wars
fuelling this
home-bound-boy's
vassalage

Embryonic history
presaging impossible
certainties.

Schrödinger's Poet

Look there!
The Sun is a spent cinder
in the gutter
concurrently
bleeding heat over my grey field

I am dead
I am alive
I am alive and dead in simultaneous, linear
combination
a macroscopic indeterminacy
a quantum absurdity

You, the observer, can reconcile
the paradox
Only you

If it can be resolved
if you need resolution

I can only remember being alive
At least I think I am alive
as I write this poem

You can decide ....

Though you may observe my death
or see news of it somewhere
or make it so

then as you read this poem you will know
I am alive
at least for you
though
I've been long boxed and shipped

I've not even thought of this
poem
since I wrote it

Too many beers, pills and lost brain cells
too many interests and contradictions
countless dead Suns

The Isles of Greece
A poem inspired by one of the same name by George Gordon Byron, Lord Byron

The Isles of Greece! The Isles of Greece
Remind me of the Isles of Greece
They are near Greece the Isles of Greece
They aren't like Paris Rome or Nice
So that is why I called this piece
The Isles of Greece! The Isle

Going Green

Go green
Save every tree
If you must eat meat
Eat me!